Collin

Series editors:

A library of g ... gn
language, an ... ix
levels of diffi ... are
all controlle ... to
Collins English Libra., ... ach
title indicate the level at which the book is ...
vocabulary of 300 words and appropriate structures, 2 : 600 wo..., 3 :
1000 words, 4 : 1500 words, 5 : 2000 words and 6 : 2500 words.

Collins English Library　Level 1

THE MAN WITH THREE FINGERS

Collins ELT

© John Tully 1987

Published in Great Britain by
William Collins Sons and Co Ltd
Glasgow G4 0NB

Printed in Great Britain by Martin's of Berwick

All rights reserved. No part of this book
may be reproduced, stored in a retrieval
system, or transmitted in any form or by
any means, electronic, mechanical, photocopying,
recording or otherwise, without the prior permission
of the Publisher.

First published in Collins English Library 1987

Reprinted: 1988

ISBN 0 00 370172 7

Illustrations by Trevor Waugh
Cover photograph by permission of Barnaby's Picture
Library
Cover design by Danny Lim

Chapter One

Two men jumped out of a car at London Airport. One of them was very tall.

"This is a big place, Harry." he said. "How can we find Sims?"

"In that building," said his friend. "This way ..."

Bert Sims was in the building. He was an old man, small and fat. He looked across to the doors. The two men came in. Bert saw them and he walked away with his back to them.

"They're looking for me. I know it!" His hand went into his coat and it came out with some pictures. "They mustn't find these. What can I do?"

He saw a bag on a chair. On the bag were the words, "Alan Heston, Hotel Europa, Rome".

Bert opened the bag. There were some clothes in it. He put the pictures under the clothes. Then he went to a telephone.

The two men looked round the room, again and again. "Can you see him?" asked the tall one.

"Over there!" said Harry. "At the telephone."

Bert talked fast on the telephone. "I put the pictures in a bag. The name on it is Alan Heston. He's going to Italy–to the Hotel Europa in Rome. You must be ready. Get the pictures and –"

Bert stopped. The two men were behind him. He put down the telephone.

"Hello, Sims," said Harry. "We want a little talk with you."

"Talk? Why?"

"About some pictures."

"I haven't got any pictures," said Bert.

"Who was that on the telephone," asked the tall man.

"My old mother. I said goodbye to her."

"You're coming with us, Sims," said Harry.

Sims went out of the building with the two men. The bag with the pictures in it was still on the chair.

Alan Heston came back to the chair with some tea. He was a young man with a happy look on his face. He opened his bag. On top of the clothes was a book, *Rome and the Romans*. He read some pages. Then he heard, "BA 504, Rome ... BA 504, Rome ..." He put the book back in the bag and got up.

At six o'clock an airport bus stopped at the Hotel Europa in Rome and Alan went into the hotel.

"You have a room for me," he said to the girl in the hotel. "My name is Heston."

There was a big man in a chair close to the window. He had a book in his hands. He heard the name "Heston" and he looked up.

"Here is the key to your room," said the girl to Alan. "It is number forty-five."

Alan walked away and the big man put the book up in front of his face. Alan saw his hands round the book. There were three fingers on one hand, not four.

Alan put the key in the door of number forty-five and opened it. He put his bag on the bed. He opened the bag and put his clothes on the bed. Then he saw the pictures.

They were pictures of a plane. It was a fighter plane. Alan looked at them again and again. "These aren't *my* pictures" he said. "Why are they in my bag?"

Chapter Two

In the morning Alan went to the Coliseum.

"A beautiful Roman building of 70 A.D.," said *Rome and the Romans*. "It had places for 50000

8

people. The Romans came here and saw animals from Africa and India. They saw men fight and die."

There were a lot of people in the Coliseum. One man, a big man, had his hands behind his back. One hand had three fingers on it, not four.

Some people went by. Alan looked again for the man with three fingers, but he was not there any more.

At midday Alan went back to the hotel. He opened the door of his room ... and stopped.

All his things were on the floor The bed things were on the floor too. His bag was open. He went to a small table by the bed and looked for his money. The money was still there.

He went to the telephone. "Whose hotel is this?" he asked. "I want to see the head man!"

A man came up to Alan's room. "I am Aldo Leone," he said. "This is my hotel."

"Some person came into my room this morning," said Alan. "Look at it now!"

"I'm very sorry, Mr Heston," said Leone. "Very, very sorry —"

"Who was it?"

"I don't know. Perhaps a man came in from the street."

"But what for? My things are still here. All my clothes—and my money!"

"That is good," said Leone. "That is very good. Please, do not talk to the police about this.

It is bad for my hotel. You can have this room for nothing. I want no money from you."

"Very well," said Alan. "I don't want the police."

That afternoon Alan went to look at the Roman Forum. He walked from end to end. Then he stopped to read *Rome and the Romans*.

"Does the book tell you about the Forum?"

Alan looked round. By him was a young woman in a red dress. She had a round, open face and big blue eyes.

"Yes, it does," said Alan. "Do you want to hear it?"

"Yes, please"

He read to her from the book. Then they walked round the Forum.

"What's your name?" he asked.

"Isabella Pinate. I live in Milan. My brother, Alberto Pinate, lives here in Rome."

"I'm Alan Heston. I'm a school teacher, from London. I'm here for a week, at the Hotel Europa."

"What do you think of Rome?"

"I like it very much. I want to see all of it."

"I want to see all of it too."

"You speak English very well."

"My mother is English."

"Please come round Rome with me," said Alan.

"Thank you," said Isabella. "It's good of you to ask me. Can we look at that building, now? That one over there."

Alan looked round. There was a man behind them. The man put his hand over his face – a hand with three fingers on it.

Alan and Isabella had dinner at a little place near the hotel.

"Do you like Italian food?" she asked.

"Yes, I do. I have Italian food in London sometimes. And I like –"

Alan stopped. There was a man at a table near the door. He had an orange in his hand ...

"Three fingers–again!" said Alan. He got up from his chair.

But the man got up too. He walked out to the street.

"What's wrong?" asked Isabella.

"It's that man!" said Alan. "I saw him at the hotel last night. I saw him at the Coliseum this morning, at the Forum this afternoon. Every place I go, he goes!"

"Perhaps he is looking at Rome too?"

"But why does he come and eat here?"

"He's not here now," said Isabella. "Eat your food."

Alan looked at the fish in front of him. Then he said, "A man came into my hotel room this morning. I was at the Coliseum. Perhaps it was

14

Three Fingers? Perhaps he saw me at the Coliseum, then he went to the hotel."

"Why?" asked Isabella.

"I don't know! All my things were still there. He wanted *something* but it wasn't in the room. So now he is coming after me again!"

After dinner they walked a long way, to the Via Borghese. Isabella stopped by a tall building, number 347.

"My brother lives here, on the 3rd floor," she said. "We must say goodnight now."

"Can I see you again tomorrow?" asked Alan.

"Yes, of course."

"What time?"

"Nine o'clock. I can come to the Hotel Europa."

Chapter Three

Alan was ready to go out at nine in the morning. Isabella came to the hotel. "Can we go to the Trevi Fountain?" she asked.

They went to look at the fountain. Alan saw people put money into the water.

"Why are they putting money in there?" he asked.

"There's an old story about the Trevi Fountain," answered Isabella. "You put money in it and some day you come back to Rome."

"I want to come back to Rome some day," said Alan. He put money into the water.

"Can you see your man with three fingers?" asked Isabella.

"No," said Alan.

"Do you know any more about him? Who is he? What does he want?"

"I don't know his name, but perhaps ... perhaps he wants the pictures"

"Pictures?"

"Some pictures of a plane. They're not my pictures. Some person put them in my bag on the way to Rome."

"Are these pictures in your room now?"

"No, they're not. I put them in a box at the hotel. I have the key to the box here, in my coat."

"What are you going to do with the pictures?"

"I'm going back to London on Sunday. Then I can find out more about those pictures. A lot more."

At one o'clock they had something to eat.

"I must go back to my brother's house now," said Isabella.

"Oh? Must you?"

"Some friends are coming to the house at two o'clock. They're going at three. Then I can see you again."

They walked to the Via Borghese and they stopped at number three hundred and forty seven.

Alan said, "I'm going to have a drink. There's a little place at the end of the street—the Cafe Venezia. You can come to the cafe at three o'clock."

"Very well," said Isabella.

Then she put her arms round him and looked into his eyes. "I like you very much, Alan," she said.

He put his arms round her. "I like you too, Isabella."

She touched the end of his nose with her finger and she went into the building.

Alan walked off down the street. He was very happy. Isabella loved him! Beautiful Isabella!

He went into the cafe. It was small and very hot. "I don't like this place," he said. "I want to walk about. I can come back at three."

He walked out of the cafe. He looked down the street ... and saw Isabella! She came out of number three hundred and forty seven and got into a small white car. The car went off fast.

"Why is she going out in a car? Where are her friends?" Alan went to number three hundred

18

and forty seven. He looked at the names by the door. There was no "Alberto Pinate" on the third floor, or on any floor.

A woman came out of the building.

"Please tell me," said Alan, "Does Alberto Pinate live in this building?"

"No," she said. "There is no man with that name here."

Questions went round in Alan's head. "Does Isabella have a brother? Perhaps her name isn't Isabella Pinate? Then who is she? Why is she telling me stories? She said 'I like you' and she put her arms round me!"

Alan put a hand in his coat. The key to the hotel box was not there!

"Perhaps she put her hand in my coat! Perhaps she has the key? Why does she want it?"

Then the answer came to him: *Because Isabella is working for Three Fingers!*

Chapter Four

Isabella stopped the white car by the Hotel Europa. She went into the hotel.

"I want to open one of your boxes, please," she said to the girl in the hotel.

"The boxes are in there," said the girl.

Isabella went into a small room. There were a lot of boxes. She looked at Alan's key. The number on it was twenty-one. She opened box twenty-one.

There was nothing in it!

"What are you doing with that box?"

Isabella looked round. Mr Leone was behind her.

"That is Mr Heston's box," he said. "His pictures are not in there any more. They are in *my* room!"

"How do you know about the pictures?" asked Isabella.

"Mr Heston telephoned ten minutes before you came here."

Isabella opened her bag. "We're going to your room," she said. "You must give the pictures to me."

She had a gun in her hand.

Alan put down the telephone in the cafe. He went out to the street. A taxi stopped in front of him.

"Hotel Europa, please," said Alan.

The white car was still in the street by the hotel. Alan jumped out of the taxi and he went into the hotel.

Leone was by the door of his room. Isabella was behind him.

"Isabella!"

She looked round. Leone walked into his room fast—and he closed the door behind him! Isabella looked at the door and at Alan. Then she walked out of the hotel.

Alan went after her. "Isabella! I must talk to you!"

But she got into her car and went off in it.

The taxi was still there. "Drive after that car!" said Alan. "I must talk to that woman."

The taxi went off after the car.

Then the driver asked a question. "Has Miss Pinate got the pictures?"

Alan's mouth opened. "What was that? The pictures! How do *you* know about...?" Then he saw the driver's hands on the wheel. There were three fingers on one of them, not four.

"It's you!" said Alan.

"Yes, it's me!"

"Who are you?"

"My name is Silva. I want the pictures, Mr Heston. Has Miss Pinate got them?"

"No, she hasn't got them!" said Alan. "Mr Leone has them at the hotel."

"Oh!" said Silva. He stopped the taxi. "We must go back to the hotel. You must ask Leone for the pictures. And you must give them to me."

"No!" said Alan. "You can't have them! I'm going to the police!" He opened the door of the taxi.

"Stop!" said Silva.

But Alan went through the door fast. He landed on the ground on his back. Then he jumped up. He saw a bus across the street, with a lot of people in it.

Alan jumped on to the bus, and its doors closed behind him.

The bus went down a long street and then over the river. Alan looked out from the back. The taxi was behind the bus.

Silva was at the wheel. His eyes looked at Alan. They were black and very cold. "You can't get away from me!" they said.

The bus stopped in front of St. Peter's. Alan looked round. Silva's taxi was not there. He looked for a policeman but there was no policeman near.

The people from the bus went into the building.

"Silva can't find me with all these people!" said Alan. He went into the building with them.

St. Peter's was very big. A man talked in English about the many rich and beautiful things. "This, of course, is by Michelangelo ... And please look at Saint Peter's Chair ..."

Alan looked for Silva, not at the chair.

"We're now going on top of the building," said the man. "Come this way, please."

It was a long way up! Then they walked out into a big open place with small buildings on it.

Alan looked for Silva again. "I can't see him," he said. "He's not here."

"We are now going to the top of *this* building," said the man. "From up there you can see all of Rome. Please come with me."

The people went into a tall building with a round top. Alan walked by a small building on the top of St. Peter's and looked down to the ground. There were people down there, very small. "I can't see Silva," he said. "Where is he now?"

"I am here, Mr Heston."

Silva came from behind the small building.

Chapter Five

Silva stopped in front of Alan.

"Now we can talk," he said. "Those people can't see us or hear us."

"Go away from me!" said Alan. "You can't have the pictures. I can tell you now ..."

"No!" said Silva. "*I* can tell *you* something. It is a very sad story. It is about a young man. He is standing on top of a tall building. And then –

one, two – over he goes! He lands on the ground. People run across to him. They want to help him, but they can do nothing. The poor man is dead! They look up at the building but they see nothing. Perhaps the young man jumped from the top because he wanted to die?"

"You are going to kill me?" said Alan. "Why? You can't get the pictures from the hotel."

"Oh, yes I can! I can say to Mr Leone, 'I am Alan's father. My poor boy is dead.' 'I am very sorry,' says Leone. 'Very, very sorry!' Then I say, 'Please give me his things.' So he gives me your clothes, your bag ... *and the pictures!*"

Alan's face was very white. The end of the building was behind him. Silva was in front of him. There was no help for him!

Silva's long arms came up.

"No!" said Alan. "No ...!"

Silva put a hand over Alan's face. Alan went back ... and back ...

"Goodbye, Mr Heston!" said Silva.

And then ... Silva's mouth opened. His arms went up in the air and his legs went from under him. He landed at Alan's feet.

He was dead!

Alan looked down at him. Then he looked up – and saw Isabella. She had her gun in her hand.

"You killed him!" said Alan.

"Yes," she said. "Because he was ready to kill you."

"What are you doing here?" asked Alan.

"I saw you and Silva in the taxi, behind my car. Then you ran to the bus. I came after you."

"But why? Aren't you working for him?"

"Of course not!" said Isabella. "I'm working for the British."

The police talked to Alan and Isabella for a long time. Men came from the British Embassy in Rome and they talked to the police.

Then the police said to Alan, "You can go now."

"And Miss Pinate?" he asked.

"She can go too."

The Embassy men went with Alan to the Hotel Europa. "Please give the pictures to us," they said.

Alan asked Leone for the pictures and the men went away with them.

That night Isabella came to the hotel.

"What is it all about?" asked Alan. "Who put those pictures in my bag?"

"A man at London Airport," said Isabella. "His name is Bert Sims. He put the pictures in your bag because our men were there too. Then he telephoned Silva in Rome. That night our people asked Sims a lot of questions. I know because I was with them. At the end of it, Sims talked. And I came to Rome."

"Because you wanted the pictures?"

"Yes."

"You said nothing about this to me! Why not?"

"Because they're pictures of a new fighter plane. People musn't know about the plane. Or about *me*. Or about my work."

"I know now!" said Alan.

"Oh yes, you know now. A lot of people know now!" Isabella was very sad. "I can't do this work any more."

Alan was sad too. "I liked you very much, Isabella. I still do. But for you it was all a chapter in a story, wasn't it?"

She put her hand on his. "I'm at the end of that chapter. Now I must begin a new one. Do you still want to see Rome – with me?"

"Yes, I do!" said Alan.

A Game with Words

Here is a word game. There are 18 questions. All the answers come from the story. Write every answer at its number on page 32. Read the letters in the boxes marked by the arrows, *down* the page. They make a question. Can you answer it?

1 How many men jumped out of the car at London Airport?

2 Who said "You're coming with us, Sims"?

3 What was the number of Alan's room at the hotel?

4 Alan said, "I'm here for a _____."

5 Trevi is the name of a _____.

6 Alan said, "I'm going back to London on _____.

7 Isabella's car was red/white/yellow/green? Which?

8 The cafe was small and very _____.

9 Isabella said her brother's name was _____.

10 What was the number of Alan's box at the hotel?

11 Alan put down the _____ in the cafe.

12 Alan said to the taxi driver, "Drive _____ that car!"

13 Sims put some _____ in Alan's bag.

14 The bus doors closed _____ Alan.

15 Alan landed on his back on the _____!

31

16 The bus went down a long _____.

17 Isabella was working for the _____.

18 At the end of the story Isabella was _____.

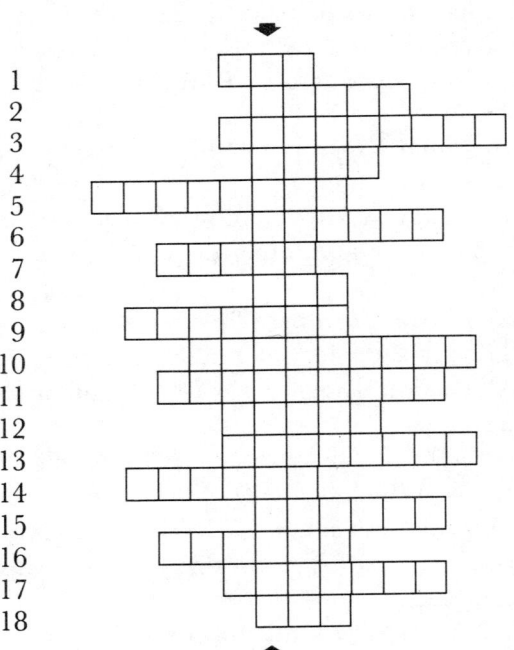